A Million Visions of Peace

Wisdom from the Friends of Old Turtle

Jennifer Garrison   Andrew Tubesing

A Million Visions of Peace

Wisdom from the Friends of Old Turtle

Pfeifer-Hamilton
Duluth, Minnesota

Pfeifer-Hamilton Publishers
210 West Michigan Street
Duluth MN 55802-1908
218-727-0500

A Million Visions of Peace:
Wisdom from the Friends of Old Turtle

"Voices of Peace" text and music © 1995 Dyan Fanning White

Printed by Dong-A Publishing and Printing Co. Ltd.
10 9 8 7 6 5 4 3 2 1

Editorial Director: Susan Gustafson
Art and Design: Jeff Brownell, Joy Morgan Dey

Cover art: Angie Fritz

Library of Congress Cataloging in Publication Data
95-69777

ISBN 1-57025-079-0
Printed in the Republic of Korea

Dedicated to our parents
and
to all the peacemakers whose
lives inspire others

JLG & ADT

Publisher's Preface

When we published the book *Old Turtle* in 1992, we knew it was special, even magical. We believed so wholeheartedly in its lyrical message of compassion and respect for all people that, from the beginning, we chose to commit one percent of the revenues to peacemaking and environmental projects.

The overwhelming response to *Old Turtle* challenged us to make new commitments to peacemaking. And so the Old Turtle Peace Project was born. We began by offering grants to communities for local peacemaking events and projects.

We also sent Old Turtle on the road to spread the word and encourage the envisioning process. A 1975 VW Beetle™ (painted to look like Old Turtle herself), accompanied by peace educators, Jennifer Garrison and Andrew Tubesing, traveled across the United States for nearly a year. Young and old gathered in schools, churches, libraries, bookstores, and community centers to share their own visions of peace.

We soon realized that millions of people had been touched by the message of the Old Turtle Peace Project.

As the project gained momentum, it became clear that people of all ages are yearning for peace in their homes and schools, in their neighborhoods and throughout the world. They are eager to become peacemakers themselves and fervently hope they can influence the world's leaders to embrace peaceful approaches to conflict We gathered their visions of peace for delivery to the United Nations.

From the hundreds of thousands of heartfelt messages we received, Jennifer and Andrew selected over two hundred that express the longing of Americans everywhere for a more peaceful world.

We hope these messages will nurture your own vision of peace and that you, in turn, will inspire others by living out your vision.

—The Publishers

ur country needs more peace among the people who liv

erybody in the world, no matter if they're a different color, they should be g

gether in harmony **if all people accepted one ano**

together why fight over little things like what religon people are, what co

ryone comes together **all people have equal right**

hands smiling and singing **all humanity helps one anoth**

being prejudiced people of all kinds *people are*

akes the world brighter *peace to all people* **peace betwe**

ice *be a hero* really discuss **person by person, becoming just "we"**

one nation **our world** community *for blacks and white*

ntries and races really get along **talk first!** we should help ea

ear the voices of the oppressed *all nations and beings helping*

ther people *be nice* help each other throughout the world **th**

and loving to each other **peace is love, love is friendship**

ple if they're different love one another everyone a quiet

st friend sandwich hugs for everybody **shake ha**

ve harmony and balance *respect for one another* my visic

d safety the human race can live in harmony **be**

qual **you have no right to hate** *my vision for peace is space technolog*

With love-joined hands

—Marcy, Iowa

We all have friends about whom we care deeply. Before we knew them, they were outsiders, but they had the potential to join our circle of friends. If we recognize that each person in the world is only a handshake and a smile away from becoming our friend, then we know that there are no outsiders. We are all members of a single worldwide community.

Be nice to each other.

—Jailyn

My vision for peace is a world where it doesn't matter if you're a **Boy** or **Girl**

—Dylan

—Dylan, Ohio

Peace *begins in each person's* **heart** *and then is passed on to the people they* love *most. Then they pass it on until* everyone *has peace in their heart.*

—Patricia, Minnesota

—Nicole, Ohio

—Christa, 8, New York

—Carrie, 10, Illinois

PEACE is accepting one another for what we are. PEACE is learning. It also is listening to what people have to say with an open mind.

—Judy, Iowa

Dear U.N.

I want world peace because all the fighting going on is just not solving anything. So many have died because of war and need for power. I mean how would you feel if your family or a friend died in a war? I bet not very good. How would you feel if on the news or from people all you heard was about killings and stuff?

Now what are you going to do about it?

—Sean, 11, Illinios

—Pam, 6th grade, Missouri

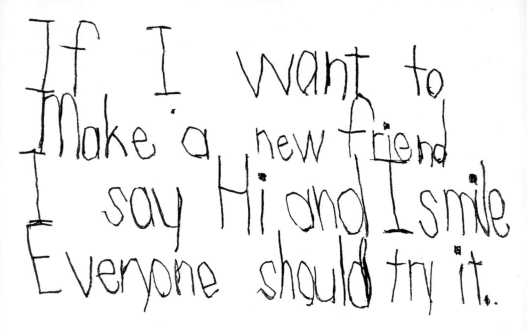

If I want to make a new friend I say Hi and I smile Everyone should try it.

—Mark, 6, Wisconsin

—Unknown

—Krista, New York

Make friends with someone who's lonely and care about them

—Derryn, 2nd grade, Michigan

A peaceful bunch!!!

—Nicole 12, New York

World of Peace

—Lisa, Missouri

—Unknown, Virginia

To start trying to make peace in this world,
I can start by first trying to make peace in my class.
I can stop hanging out with people who
make fun of others.
I think people in my class should stop being so
exclusive and be more inclusive.

—Jackie, 13, Missouri

no more
clucux clams,

—Alex

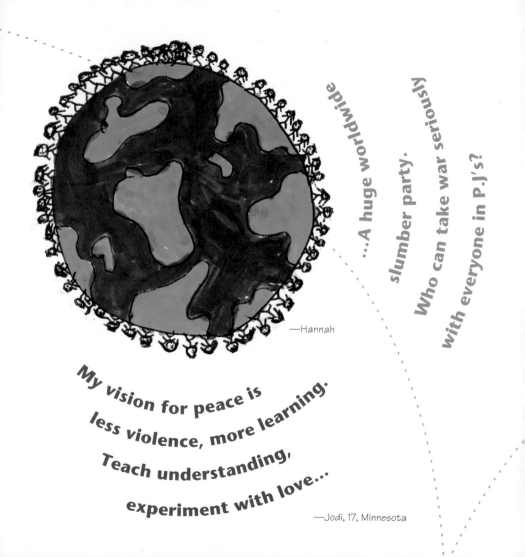

...A huge worldwide slumber party. Who can take war seriously with everyone in P.J's?

—Hannah

My vision for peace is less violence, more learning. Teach understanding, experiment with love...

—Jodi, 17, Minnesota

World peace to me would be a contiguous flow of love between nations, races, and people. In my head I can see this picture!

With love-joined hands we can do anything!

—Marcy, 14, Iowa

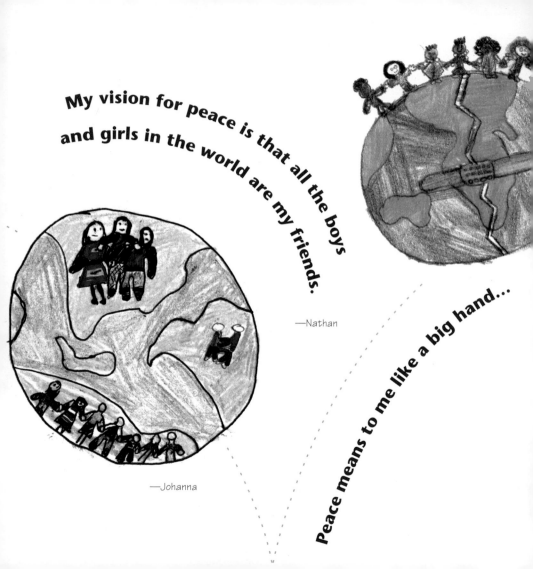

My vision for peace is that all the boys and girls in the world are my friends.

—Nathan

—Johanna

Peace means to me like a big hand...

...and each finger is a different country.

—Dustin, 8, Pennsylvania

—Natasha, 12, New York

—Amy, 2nd grade, Oregon

—Angie, 13, Ohio

$\mathcal{G}$od made the world for us to share,

So we need to show him that we care.

Hand in hand we all should be,

Living together in harmony.

We need to correct our mistakes today,

Before our Earth fades away.

—Danah, Iowa

—Monica

One time the tiger wanted to dance with somebody. Then he found the turtle. The turtle thought the tiger would eat him. But the tiger said, "I only want to dance with you." "Yes" said turtle. And they danced.

—Marriam, 6, Minnesota

—Nasreen, 12, Ohio

What can I do to be a member of the global village?
Ideas for friends of Old Turtle

- Learn about the United Nations and its mission.
- Sing the songs and read the poetry and folk tales of other cultures.
- Get to know a person from another country or another community.
- Learn a new language.
- Write to a pen pal from another country that you would like to visit.
- Celebrate holidays of other ethnic and religious groups.

verybody throw garbage in the garbage can you v
up our earth recycle your trash stop cutting dow
recyclable stuff clean up the world **plant flowers** m
earth **ride bikes more than cars** don't get pollution
iggy if animals don't have a habitat, they can't live **do**
ash there should be a fine if you litter **we nee**
reuse plastic cups we want to save the world the wor
people are dying because there is no food help a
animals deserve respect solar power **be aware** I am goi
top throwing trash in the water help the f
heir children environmental values manufacture goods
cycle paper **animals need trees** *no more deers*
world's cry for help stop polluting *this is our world* I wa
ature litter in the ocean will kill the sea animals **there wi**
orest trees are getting cut down **many animals die** sto
erious water is one of our our most impor
o litter more trees make a turtle happy. don't litter set
l animals *be nice to the dinosaurs* **I wish the world**
ecycled paper for school workbooks *make safe e*

We only get one earth

—Diana, 4th grade

All over America, kids are challenging adults to take better care of the earth. Youth are taking the lead, asking their elders to make sacrifices that will protect the environment. Very soon, these young people who are already dedicated to preserving the earth will become its leaders. Their commitment paints a hopeful picture for the planet we share.

—Unknown

Peace is a river, cool and calm.
On a snow covered mountain,
with a red sun behind it.
Peace is beautiful,
peace is everywhere.

—Joey

Katie, Kentucky

Everybody is the same as animals.

You don't have to treat animals bad because it hurts them.

We should treat the Earth good not bad because we don't get another Earth to live on.

Keep this Earth clean we only get one Earth, no more.

—Diana, 4th grade

I would like to see a world
in which there is a reverence
for all forms of life. Where animals are not
used and abused and
there is a greater concern
for the environment.

—Jean, 28, Maryland

—Unknown, Michigan

My vision for peace . . .

PICKING UP LITTER
OUT OF A DEAD FOREST

—Megan, 7, Pennsylvania

—Sarah, 10, New Hampshire

Stop hunting Endangered animals!

—David, 8, Minnesota

Rainforest	you were a lovely, beautiful forest
Rainforest	you were still, dense, and full of life
Rainforest	you were everything a forest animal needed
Rainforest	we ruined you by cutting you down
Rainforest	but we can fix it by planting more trees for you

—Emily, 12, Michigan

I would like to see the rainforest live forever.

—Ashton

—Jamie, 10, Iowa

if you dont help clean up
the anamals will die

—Jeremy, 7, New York

The trees, rocks, turtles, and fish.
Peace is the thing, they all wish.
Same for the ocean, sun, clouds, and wind.
To them, they all say, they are kin.
Be nice to each other, instead of starting wars,
'Cause peace is the key that will open all doors.

—John, Georgia

Megan, 9, Michigan

My wish for peace is that no one hurts crocodiles or frogs...

—Stephen, 4, Wisconsin

...or birds or lions.

—Dan, 4, Wisconsin

—Lisa, 10, New Hampshire

My vision for peace . . . is to make a car that runs on water!

water

gas

—Unknown, Michigan

I wish they would hurry up with the electric cars

I also wish people would not throw trash in the bayous

—Angie, 8, Texas

MY vision for **PEACE** is a world where everybody takes what they **NEED** and **GIVES BACK** twice as much.

—Jennifer, 10, Ontario

—Vanessa, 9, Iowa

If we respect our world now,
the world of the future
will be a world of peace.

We will have clean air
and blue skies.

—Kate, Virginia

We have to remember to keep the Earth clean because the Earth does not belong to us, we belong to the Earth

—Rebekah, 0, Florida

—Kenneth, 0, Guam

Dear United Nations Members,

My sister and I go down the road every week and pick up trash every week. I think the world should pick up trash every week just like us. I think that would be a good way to make peace.

—Dan, 9, New York

—Amanda, 9, Illinois

What can I do to become an Earth keeper?
Ideas for friends of Old Turtle

♦ Develop an intimate relationship with a park, field, or forest near your home.

♦ Grow some of your own food.

♦ Buy organic food that has been grown without pesticides.

♦ Walk or ride a bicycle instead of driving.

♦ Volunteer at your local humane society.

♦ Compost your garbage.

♦ Organize a trash pick-up at your local park.

♦ Recyle in your home, school, and place of work.

hope there will be less fighting on the playground

make our world safer all gangs come together don't f

name another kid is dead in this sad little town find ways

why can't they get along? I saw a 16 year old

cary uniforms stop using guns we should not figl

n Leanigraska people should not be in gangs elimina

for world peace because if you don't another world war might start

vars please stop your wars, they hurt and kill and accomplisl

afe all my life my cousin got shot in a driveby war is just a

going to happen to us? no war stop wars before they happen

ends soldiers march and shoot their guns war is e

tare you in the face yet hide in the corner it is nc

was affected by a murder the world is a drea

comes here? almost everybody is at war I watch on the n

ask, why do people have wars? my peace will be I will not punch r

would want to be brought up in a war s

meone is different not all problems need to be settled with war

rong with world today a gun isn't any fun it wou

ives stop having wars everyone put their guns down w

Shells are for turtles not for guns

—Mariko, Oregon

Many people live in relative safety, but for others, violence is a daily reality. All of us share a world that seems constantly to be on the brink of war. But there is hope. Just as violence spreads from one person to the next, so does peace. If we dedicate ourselves to settling our differences without violence, peace will pass from person to person until it surrounds the earth.

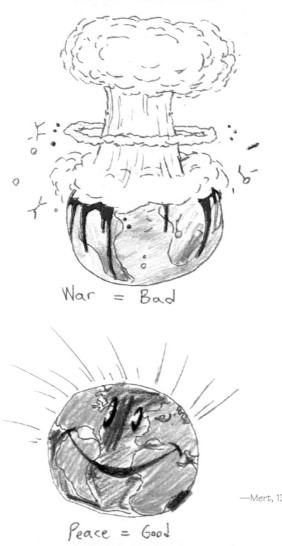

War = Bad

Peace = Good

—Mert, 13, Iowa

Your hate is boiling up inside,
It has no place to run and hide.

Your heart is breaking clean in two,
There's nothing anyone can do.

Your soul becomes a lake on fire,
To hurt someone is your desire.

You want someone to feel the pain,
That's almost driving you insane.

Then you look up so silently,
Into the eyes of your enemy.

And instead of ugly, mocking glares,
You see your pain reflected there.

— Martine, Massachusetts

My vision for PEACE is that there will be no more bullying on the PLAYGROUND

And NOT so many FIGHTS

—Kristofer, Maryland

—Jason

I wish that the people across the street will stop shooting people and stop throwing beer bottles.

—Lillian, 7, Ohio

I want it all to stop. In my neighborhood sometimes I hear gunshots and people scream almost everyday.

—Sheila, Illinois

Less violence on TV and in video games.

—Natalie, 8, Illinois

—Jamie, Minnesota

My vision for peace is that people around the world live in harmony so dads and moms wouldn't have to go to war. I missed my dad when he went to Zagreb as a peacekeeper and took care of people hurt in the war.

—Bridget Ann, 9

My Papa fot in the war. And
he got shot but did not die. He
got shot in the hart did not die in
the war but one day he cood not
reatch hes hart pils and bie. So
thats why I wish for peson
Earth.

P.S I miss My papa

—Kayde, 8, Oklahoma

Kathy Ross's students at Ockerman Middle School in Florence, Kentucky, had never given much thought to world peace until one of their classmates told them about her own experience. This is Alenka's story, as told by Alenka and her friends.

Dear United Nations,

Alenka   **I am writing this letter with hopes and dreams of peace.**

Alex   This letter may be important to you.

Daniel   I am sending this letter to ask you to try a little bit harder to work for peace.

David   Every time you turn on the television, there is something about war on.

Rodney   If we had more peace, our world would be much better.

Matt   There is a new girl in our class from war-torn Bosnia and her name is Alenka. I was very sad when she expressed her feelings in class.

John   Her story is very tragic.

Emily   Do you know what it's like for an eleven-year-old girl from Bosnia to wake up in the middle of the night thinking she heard a bomb? I do.

Sara   When she started talking about her family and country, I was shocked.

Sarah   She's made me want to do more for world peace.

Alenka   **In the war I have seen people's destroyed lives and homes. It just hurts me deep in my heart when I remember all that.**

Nicole   Before the war, Alenka and her family were living average lives, but when the war came everything changed. She became poor.

Danny   Her family ate only once a day. Her life has been very hard.

Ashley	Her dad was in a concentration camp.
Sabrina	She grew in the fighting until she moved here.
Alisha	She and her mother, father, and sister are the only ones who made it out. Some of the family died and they do not know where or what happened to the others.
Tabatha	Her aunts, uncles, and cousins are in Bosnia, and she doesn't know where they are. If she found them she would be the happiest girl in the world.
Alisha	She cannot forget the bombings and shootings.
Noah	She can't go to sleep without hearing the sound of bombs.
Alan	Sometimes when we talk to her about it she starts to cry.
Nicole	Please stop wars—they wreck people's lives and no person wants to live as Alenka did.
Alenka	**Helping is the only way to bring peace in this world.**
Lindsay	Is there anything my classmates and I can do to help?
Stephanie	Tell me how I can help.
Maggie	There may not be peace for a long time, but we can start now.
Emily	It's our future we're talking about.
Candice	Peace is a gift.
John	So please … peace.

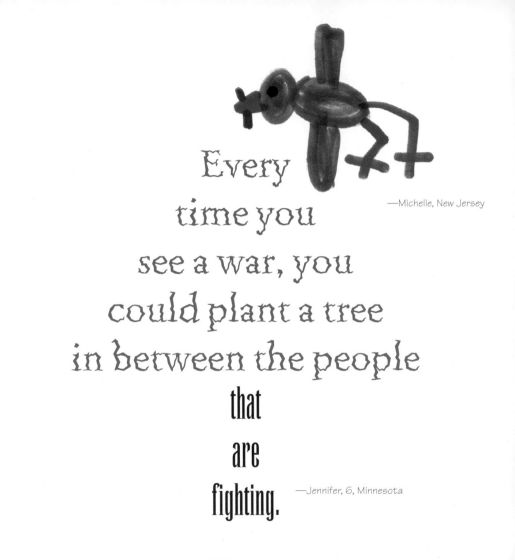

Every
time you
see a war, you
could plant a tree
in between the people
that
are
fighting.

—Michelle, New Jersey

—Jennifer, 6, Minnesota

Instead of having wars about different thoughts we could just flip a coin.

—Matt, Wisconsin

If I were in charge I would settle it over a video game!

—Alex, Oregon

We already have missionaries that spread the word about God. Maybe we can have missionaries that spread the word about peace in places where they are having wars.

—Shaina, 10, North Carolina

—Kim, 12, Ohio

—Katherine

My vision for peace . . .

is if everyone would think of
of themselves as dinosaurs
and if we keep fighting
we will soon be extinct

—Erik, 11, Minnesota

Every day when I go to school
I get scared because of violence.
I don't think it's fair that I have
to be scared. I fear the day that
I will have to face a gang.
I hope that with your help I
will not have face that day.

—Clare

Gang members go to other neighborhoods and make trouble with other gangs. And little kids like 9-10 years old see us in gangs and they want to be like us and do the things we're doing so we need peace to show the little ones.

—Tray, Oregon

—Aaron, 12, Utah

THe BomB
shouLD Be STOPPeo

—Mugsie, Wisconsin

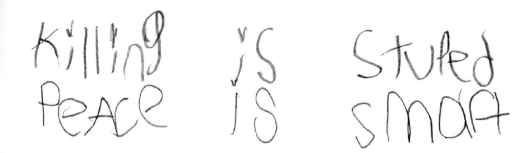

Killing
PeaCe

is
is

Stuped
smart

—Jon, 7

SHELLS FOR TURTLES NOT FOR GUNS!

—Mariko, Oregon

—Andrea, 12, Kentucky

Erase The
Violence

—Luke, 5th grade

My vision for peace is that I want to be able to walk through the halls and not have to chase my books and pencils around the floor when the eighth graders knock them out of my hand.

I also wish there had never been war.

—Aaron

—James, New York

I don't want people to Die.

—Dakota, Oklahoma

We want peace so no more little children have to die.

—Brittney, 6, Florida

No more wars!

—Asha, 1st grade, Minnesota

—Erin, New Hampshire

—Erin, 10, Ohio

War: (wör), *n.* may it be a word that future generations have to look up in the dictionary.

—Jeanne, Minnesota

*I dream to be a person who cares
for the world. It aches me that
I'm writing and something bad is
happening right now.*

—Carey, 11, Pennsylvania

No raping in the
whole wide world
mostly to little girls
and women.

—Valerie, Michigan

That we would never

have to look over our

shoulders in fear...

...Footsteps behind

us would only mean

friendly company.

—Unknown

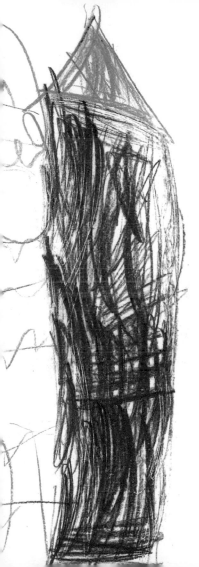

Hello, This picture is a girl who lives in peace.

She likes to play.

She isn't scared.

I'd like the world to be this way.

—Caleb, 6, Nebraska

we must stop the wars and the fights. we need to learn to communicate by using words instead of weapons.

—David, 7

—Unknown

What can I do to prevent violence?

Ideas for friends of Old Turtle

- When you feel angry:
  - Take a deep breath
  - Count to ten
  - Use words
  - Walk away
- Lobby for violence prevention programs at school
- If you can't resolve a conflict, ask someone to help.
- Learn about the places in your community and world that are troubled by violence.
- Volunteer at a safe house for battered women.
- Turn off violent TV programs.

everyone will laugh don't buy drugs more re

nrise peace starts with one person—you peace is like you

taking a bubble bath **reading** eat sleep play

ocolate chip cookies an angel keep the spirit of Christm

ing to temple **good vibes coming from within** inn

sitting on the front porch watching kids play

ers kids should feel safe **we have enough streng**

ccept each other **hope** peace be with you embra

conditional love compassion for all living things peace

their hearts **learn** stop doing drugs take tir

n children would not have to be afraid **be you**

a tree **peace is quiet, soft, gentle** it's not turr

preads listen peace in the hearts of all people peace

e problems with reasoning, not bullets **quiet and** c

happy about who you are calmness have a clea

ace in our community deep silent sleep admit y

t change ourselves get along believe in God **I w**

e ourselves in others **people accept each o**

lm peace is something we need in my tr

Peace in our hearts

—Michael, Washington

It's tough to be a peacemaker if you aren't first at peace with yourself. People find inner peace in many ways: by praying or meditating, by painting or writing poetry, by hiking or sailing, by talking with friends or keeping a journal. If you create a peaceful place within your heart, you will find the inner resources to become a more effective peacemaker in your community.

Be a pese
Marr. and be Pestol,

—Unknown

Peace as an Eagle

I love to feel peace

The peace I feel as I watch

   Eagle soaring in the air

The peace of the water shimmering in the lake

The peace of deer hiding in the trees

The peace of coyote racing across the plains

The peace of the mountain rising into the sky

And as I look higher, again I see Eagle

   soaring above the mountains

And this brings me peace.

—Jacob, 11, Washington

Let us all strive for peace in our own hearts . . .

—Adam, 10, Kansas

Then watch it spread like Sunrise over a newly awakened world.

—Michael, Washington

playing basketball with my friends

—Kristopher, 7, Texas

I play baskitball and tag.
I play thes things Fare.
IF i AM it i WELL NOT Liy.

—Chris, 3rd grade

My wish for peace is
that no other people in
my family will get

DIVORCED

—Shelley, 8, California

—Unknown

When I sit upon a
riverstream and cast
my line, I sit down
on waters edge It is
Peacefull to be
alone

—Brad, 3rd grade, Michigan

When we step back and recapture
what around us is truly awe-inspiring
—like babies and sunsets and storms and
rivers and life and art and bird music—
then we will feel enough love for our world
not to want it violated, by non-peace, by violence.
There is a way to truly love our world,
that is to rediscover its wonder.

—Erin, New York

—Unknown

If you watch a butterfly
with someone you don't know
then you can both enjoy it
and start to be friends

—Patricia Dahl's class, Washington

—Ashley

I do not think this world will ever find peace.

The only way I believe this world or people
will ever find peace is in death.

Then people have no more worries,
they hear of or see no more death.

I really hope there is such a thing as heaven.

—Max, teen, Oregon

MY wish for peace is to have less crime and
to help the endangered species a lot.
I, as an 11 Year old, know that it can be hard
out there. I've had to go out on the streets
and be poor with mY mom and I would't want
any child to go through what I did.

—Janie, 11, Texas

Peace is having **no one** to fight with because no one has made you want to fight.

Peace is living without worry because you have nothing to worry about.

Peace is having **no one** to put down because you feel good enough about yourself.

—Johnny, 13, Washington

There would be peace if everyone would listen to their angel.

—Mitchell, 7, Ohio

—Emily, 8, Michigan

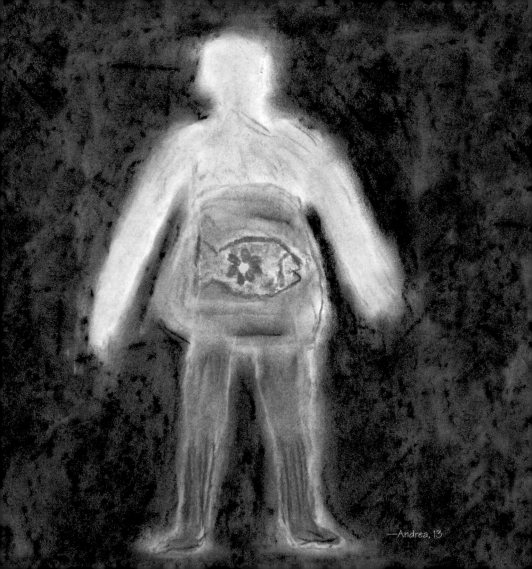

—Andrea, 13

My wish is for people to undertake the cleaning of the windows of the soul.

Centuries of grime and self-deception cloud inner revelation.

Only by truly cultivating deep inner awareness, will inner peace become attainable.

Once a certain critical point of individuals working toward this common goal is attained, then external events will follow suit.

—Cheri, Michigan

Shield Shield Shield Shield Shield Shield Shield Shield Shield

World Peace World Peace World Peace World Peace World Peace World Peace World Peace World

—Jason, 13, Virginia

—Elizabeth, Texas

Peace is running home to my mom.

—Roy, 3rd grade, Michigan

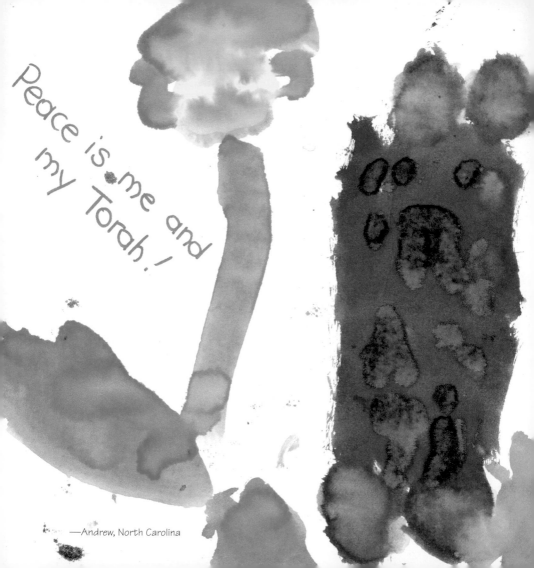

Peace is me and my Torah!

—Andrew, North Carolina

When the people came they had no peace.
But when they saw God in the people's eyes
they had peace.

—Niki, Kentucky

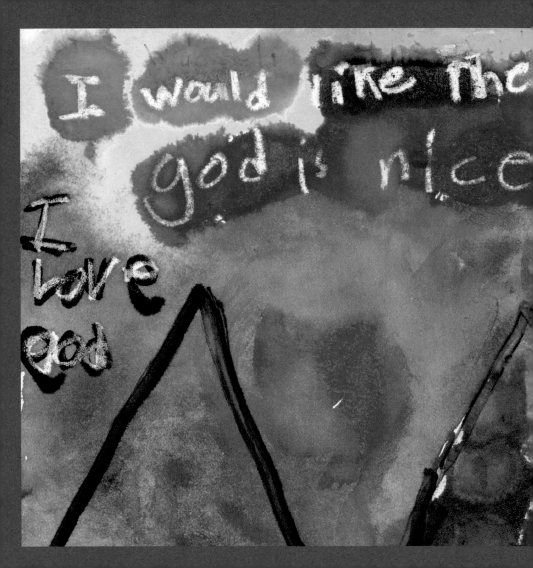

w word to be nice

—Tiffany, 7, Hawaii

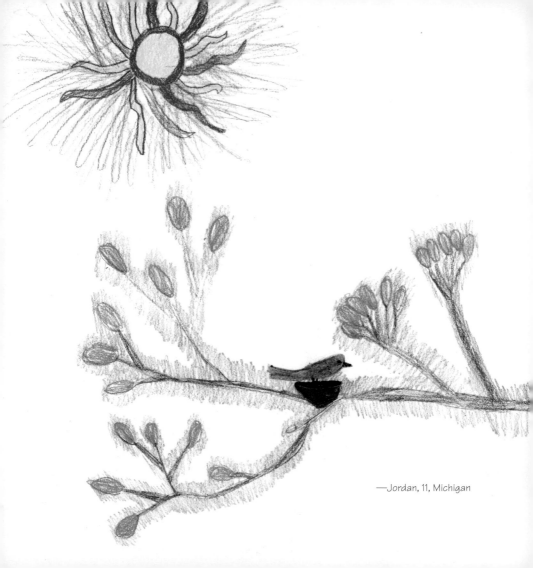

—Jordan, 11, Michigan

Peace

Peace is everything to me.

It's the things I hear and the things I see.

It's the evening birds and their chirping sounds,

And they can be heard all around.

It's as calm as the evening breeze.

I love the rivers that flow and the great green trees.

Peace is lovely to me.

—April, 10, Georgia

—Christine, 10, Ohio

World peace starts with one person. I will start; will you help me to continue?

—Ann, 12, Pennsylvania

—Danielle, Michigan

What can I do to find inner peace?
Ideas for friends of Old Turtle

♦ Keep a Joy Journal in which you record at least one thing that makes you happy each day.

♦ Take time for rest and sleep so you are refreshed and ready to meet the challenges of each new day.

♦ Enjoy the company of a good book.

♦ Remember what you do well.

♦ Pray or meditate.

♦ Find a hobby you love and take time to do it.

♦ Renew your energy in the outdoors.

irds and bees and apple trees **barn yard animals all aro**

sunny day **birds flying around me** less peopl

side silence sharing with another child helping starv

one step at a time peace is green, peace is the gras

saying please and thank you a smile on your

ters bed peaceful chaos, blissful discord no more r

being good and delightful **we will be happy** see

ild and speak with hope for the future paint good

e world always keep your balance **revolutioniz**

field eating grass not being scared peace is son

uge, freedom **a treehouse** peace is life, peace i

living for first world nations who gladly share thei

zar no cigars, no beating, no secrets, no stealing, no violen

hope **aid refugees of war before they all perish** do

ter when she has a cold peace is love, solid love **ignore**

eace peace is love, peace is also a flying dove, peace is a

song bird **leave everything alone the way you foun**

dance with the wind **create wishes** peace is having a

lence we made a recipe for peace, one cup of nonviolence, one and a ha

Please pass the peace

—Gregg, Minnesota

Across the United States, people are answering the question "How do we find peace?" They are not just talking, they are making peace happen. In Montana, sisters promise to share and play together. In New Mexico, young people erect a peace statue. In Massachusetts, college students gather elementary kids for a day of peace games. The next person to become a peacemaker could be a friend, a neighbor, a family member—or it could be you.

—Mike, 11, New Hampshi

Every year near Christmas you have a cease-fire all over the world for a day.

If for one day, why not for one year?

My wish is that you offer each country $2,000.00 if they can make peace and leave all their disagreements behind for one year.

And then see how they like it.

—Jerwarn, 13, Mississippi

—Annakatrin, New York

I think peace is when people and animals don't fight and everything is quiet and pretty.

I find peace when I go out onto the front porch and watch the birds fly by and the wind blow leaves on the trees around.

I hope some day that people will understand how bad we are taking care of our planet.

—Nick

Thinking of a rainbow

Christina, 6, Ohio

—Dana, Colorado

Voices of Peace

by Dyan F. White

©1995 words and music by Dyan F. White

What **peace** is to me
is **beauty** and **life**.

—Katie

1 Book for every child
In the

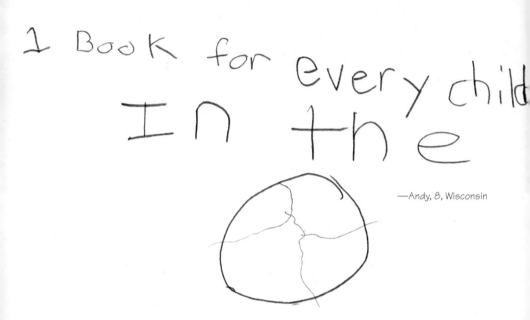

—Andy, 8, Wisconsin

My wish is for a tootsie pop.
And for everyone to have food.

—Chris, 10, New Jersey

—Allison, Texas

My Vision of peace is for the world to be fair

—Brian, Virginia

My vision for peace . . .

Would be when all children could sleep safely in their beds

—Unknown, New York

—Gregory, Minnesota

Recipe for Peace

1 cup of helping others
1/2 cup of Compromise
2 cups of friendship
4 Tbsp. of Compliments
1 cup of cooperation
2 cups of love

1/4 cup of self-esteem
2 Tbsp. of kindness
2 Tbsp. of Caring
2 Tbsp. of honesty

Directions

Mix it all together and make it often because it's all you need for a lifetime of happiness.

—Mrs. Morse's 3rd grade class, Massachusetts

I am just a kid and I know that peace is better than war.
How come the people who run the nations of the world are not as smart as I am?

—Adam, New Jersey

Look here every body, you better staighten yourself out right now or I'll send you to your room.

—Unknown, Oregon

Peace is human rights,
and no more fights.
It's love not war
that's at your door.
You must close your door to war,
and let love flow forever more.
Peace is friends right to the end
that is my trend,
and so my poem shall end.

—Kareem, New Jersey

birds love

Rabbits love

turtles love

cats love

Dogs love

fish love

Pigslove

horses love

mice love

—Jenna, 9, North Carolina

My vision for peace . . . is that there would not be war...that people would respect each others' cultures and religions... that there would be no more hunger... that there would be no more homeless people... that there would be cures for cancer and AIDS... that there would not be any suffering... that all the people on earth would love and care for one another as brothers and sisters as *God* wants us to.

—Unknown

I am of caring human flesh.
I here the sounds of wild things.
I see the world filled with many wonders!
I understand the feelings and needs of others.
I say life is not measured by years but by love.
I wish the world was like this.
I am of caring human flesh.

—Elizabeth, 12, Illinois

Peace is love
Peace is how
The wind blows
Through the grass...

—Dorcey

...Peace is how
your eyes twinkle,
or when you're old,
your skin will wrinkle.
This is peace, not war.

—Shaun, 13, California

Peace is 🕊 Peace is

Sharing.

Peace is the best
thing I've ever heard
Of.

—Bettina, Michigan

Peace is a knot being untied.

—Kaye, 3rd grade, Michigan

Peace is like a roller coaster.
First, you're nervous to try it,
but once
you try it,
you love it!

—Nick, Michigan

ARe PeoPle BeiNG
iN PeAce is GooD
BeiNG iN PeAce is
HAPPe

—Unknown

Peace is not fighting, it is loving and caring for one another

Every one is put on this earth for a reason, we are all god's gift and we should respect that with peace

Any and everybody should, no matter who you are, or how big a star, the greatest gift you can give is love

Cincinatti to China all should find peace, it does'nt matter what color skin, or what language you speak, besides, color is only skin deep

Every one must find love, but the key to finding love is finding peace.

—Timothy, 13, Virginia

—Otis, Nevada

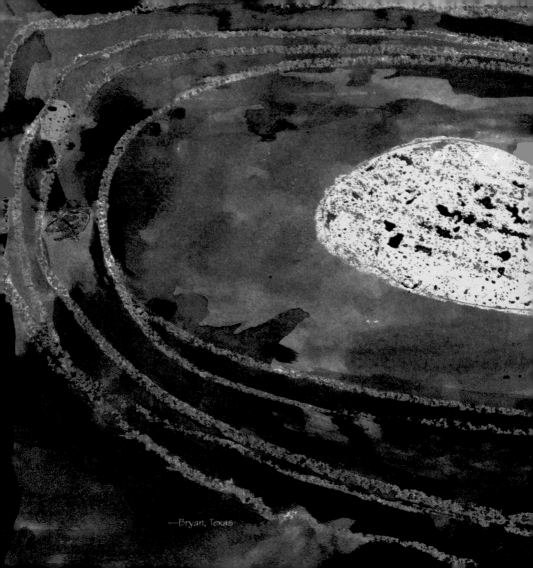
—Bryan, Texas

My vision for world peace is
internal harmony,
family harmony,
and that we each connect
one star with another
and twinkle and shine
in a galaxy dance of joy

—Sara, Iowa

—Louis, 8, Massachusetts

$\mathcal{P}$lant the seed of love today
  It's sure to circle back your way...

$\mathcal{W}$e can all watch it grow
  There it goes like dominoes...

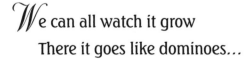

—Erica

—Jenny

*I*t will circle Mother Earth
 touching each and every birth
 So please just plant the seed today
 It's sure to circle back your way.

—Unknown, Connecticut

Peace is just a dream unless we do something

—Steve, 10, Ohio

—Jimmy, Virginia

A Million Visions of Peace

We hope the visions of peace shared on these pages have stimulated you to envision a more peaceful world.

If today you share your vision of peace with two people, and if they each share their vision with two people tomorrow, and if those four each share their vision with two more people the next day—it will take only nineteen days for a million people to envision peace. In one month, the entire population of the world will have shared a vision of peace.

Action follows vision. If you commit yourself to peaceful action today, and encourage two friends to do the same tomorrow and they each influence two more, as the process continues, the entire population of the Earth will become dedicated peacemakers in only 31 days!

With our own vision we can change our lives.

With shared vision we can change the world.

—Christa, 8, New York

Acknowledgments

We thank every school, church, bookstore, and individual who dreamed of peace and who included us in their dream by joining the Old Turtle Peace Project. Each message that we received is a unique and beautiful expression of its creator's vision for peace. We wish that we could have included them all in this book, but we had to select only a few to represent the hundreds of thousands that we received. Many peace messages were unsigned or were identified only by the author's or artist's name. If you recognize your work in this book and it is unattributed, we'd love to hear from you.

—Jennifer and Andrew

Credits

WITH LOVE-JOINED HANDS Alex, Erica, Monica, Dylan Ian Adams, Danah Allchin, Jailyn B, Derryn Beasley, Nicole Bogner, Krista Bradford, Nicole E. Butler, Sioban Case, Lisa Coerver, Johanna Cutler, Hannah Franklin, Angie Fritz, Jackie Gerard, Nasreen Ghazi, Marcy Hubbard, Carri Johnson, Judy Johnson, Marriam Khalaj, Jodi Knutson, Natasha Lauiston, Cara Miller, Nathan Miller, Christa Montani, Pam Overman, Amy Paul, Patricia Radecki, Mark Scoptur, Dustin Starer, Sean Zitzer **WE ONLY GET ONE EARTH** Diana Alvarez, Jean Boisvert, Dan Brassan, Kenneth Clark, David Carr, Lisa Douglas, Megan Filipski, Ashton J. Forley, Jennifer Fortes, Joey Gartner, Kate Ginivan, Jeremy High, Emily Hospodar, John Hudelston, Dan Lundean, Daniel L. Marsh, Rebekah Miller, Amanda Morley, Vanessa Panthen, Katie Prall, Jean Redzikowski, Megan Rochow, Jamie Sogard, Stephen Strupp, Angie Thomas **SHELLS ARE FOR TURTLES NOT FOR GUNS** Mariko, Sarah Ables, Mert Akinc, Lillian Allen, Katherine Balliew, Brittney Balliet, Shaina Birkhead, Clare Bowles, David Clank, Candice Clark, Kayde Coltharp, Tabatha Coman, Carey Cottrell, Sabrina Cragliardi, Asha Duncan, Alan Dietz, Rodney Foltz, Sheila Touche, Alex Friedman, Aaron Fredricks, Jason Giers, John H., Emily Hagedorn, Erin Hess, Sara Hollowell, Matt Hoover, Nicole Howell, Bridget Ann Keeton, Jamie Kimlinger, James Konatus, Ashley Luster, Noah Mann, Alenka Maric, Erin McDowell, John Meek, Caleb Moore, Andrea Mumme, Natalie Newberg, Kristofer Ochs, Mugsie Pike, Alisha Pratt, Martine Prentis, Danny Reed, Luke Reynolds, Kim Ross, David Routte, Tray Savage, Stephanie Scheid, Michelle Sciuto, Jeanne Seitz, Matt Simpson, Daniel Spradling, Valerie Stoneham, Erik Sweetnam, Lindsay Toebbe, Dakota W., Aaron Webb, Jennifer Whitman, Alex Williams, Maggie Zilliox **PEACE IN OUR HEARTS** Andrew, Ashley, Elizabeth, Niki Bixler, Johnny Brubaker, Janie Cartwright, Ann Ciccarelli, Michael Cogle, Patricia Dahl's class, Mitchell Derr, Christine Fram, Adam Gelroth, Jacob Groves, Chris Johnson, Tiffany Johnston, Jason King, Erin Kinney, Max Kogan, Brad Koory, Cheri Lesaukis, Roy Leukus, Andrea Lonis, Emily Miller, Kristopher Riemer, Jordan Gadbaw Semer, April Smith, Shelley Smith, Danielle Zimmerman-Tiedec **PLEASE PASS THE PEACE** Annakatrin, Dorcey, Louis Auciello, Gregory Barnier, Andy Bates, Mike Cox, Adam Culbertson, Jimmy Donahue, Chris Fusco, Otis Handjoe, Kaye Hilminen, Elizabeth Hohenberger, Bettina Huntenburg, Nick Kilgren, Timothy King, Alison Krebs, Jerwarn LeSueur, Shaun MacMullan, Christina Mitchell, Mrs. Morse's 3rd grade class, Nick Neill, Bryan Olivares, Katie Perry, Steve Primeau, Brian Soule, Sara Star, Jenna Rose Valley, Kareem Wahlgren, Dyan Fanning White, Dana Wise

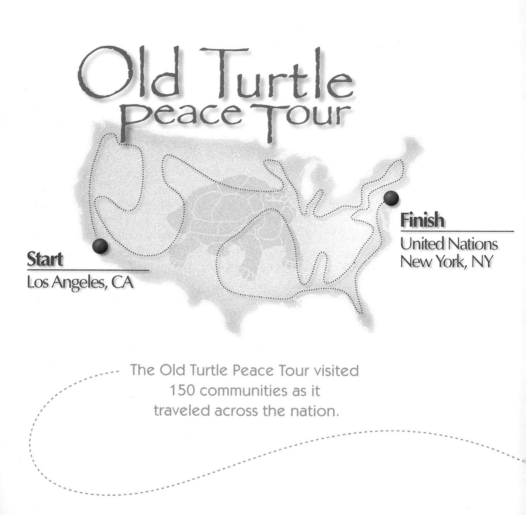

Old Turtle
Peace Tour

Start
Los Angeles, CA

Finish
United Nations
New York, NY

The Old Turtle Peace Tour visited
150 communities as it
traveled across the nation.

Old Turtle Peace Tour stops

Portland OR, Vacouver WA, Seattle WA, Kirkland WA, Olympia WA, Kent WA, Leavenworth WA, Yakima WA, Twin Falls ID, Orem UT, Salt Lake City UT, LaFayette CA, Fremont CA, San Jose CA, Los Altos CA, Soquel CA, Laguna Niguel CA, Ventura CA, Las Vegas NV, Scottsdale AZ, Tempe AZ, Ruidoso NM, Albuquerque NM, Colorado Springs CO, Aurora CO, Denver CO, Lakewood CO, Big Sky MT, Sheridan WY, Rapid City SD, Fargo ND, Faribault MN, Winona MN, Sparta WI, La Crosse WI, Stillwater MN, Hudson WI, Minneapolis MN, Wayzata MN, St. Paul MN, St. Cloud MN, Spooner WI, Rice Lake WI, Bemidji MN, International Falls MN, Duluth MN, Grand Marais MN, Eagle Harbor MI, Sister Bay WI, Milwaukee WI, Brookfield WI, Madison WI, Janesville WI, Lake Geneva WI, St. Charles IL, Oak Park IL, Buffalo Grove IL, Goshen IN, Marshall MI, Grand Rapids MI, Charlevoix MI, Indianapolis IN, Bloomington IN, Fort Thomas KY, Loveland OH, Cincinnati OH, Dayton OH, Columbus OH, Zainesville OH, Middleburg Heights OH, Rocky River OH, Pittsburg PA, Medina NY, Cooperstown NY, Northampton MA, Winooski VT, Lincoln NH, Meredith NH, Southwest Harbor ME, Brunswick ME, Danvers MA, Marshfield MA, Providence RI, Storrs CT, Greenwich CT, Port Washington NY, Stone Harbor NJ, Ridgewood NJ, Haverford PA, Narberth PA, Stratford PA, Bel Air MD, Ellicott City MD, Mechanicsburg PA, Williamsport PA, Port Chester NY, White Plains NY, Greenvale NY, Wilmington DE, Reston VA, Alexandria VA, Charlottesville VA, Harper's Ferry WV, Leesburg VA, Wake Forest NC, Charlotte NC, Montreat NC, Greenville SC, Athens GA, Roswell GA, Knoxville TN, Nashville TN, Memphis TN, Blytheville AR, St. Louis MO, Alton IL, Muscatine IA, Des Moines IA, Ames IA, Omaha NE, Kansas City MO, Manhattan KS, Newton KS, Winfield KS, Tulsa OK, Oklahoma City OK, Ardmore OK, Fort Worth TX, Dallas TX, Houston TX, Friendswood TX, Galveston TX, Longview TX, New Orleans LA, Ocean Springs MS, Mobile AL, Lakeland FL, Orlando FL

The next step

The leaders of the world need to know your ideas, hopes, and plans. Write or draw your peace vision and send it to your legislators, the president, or the secretary general of the United Nations.

If you want to learn more about peacemaking, we'd be happy to send you *Let's Be Peacemakers*, a booklet full of ideas for creating peaceful action with kids or adults, in groups or classes. To receive your free copy, write to the Old Turtle Peace Project, Pfeifer-Hamilton Publishers, 210 West Michigan, Duluth, MN 55802-1908.

Old Turtle

Text by Douglas Wood
Watercolors by Cheng-Khee Chee

Old Turtle by Douglas Wood $17.95

Old Turtle products

Old Turtle Peace Journal $12.95

Old Turtle T-Shirts (Child M, L, Adult M, L, XL, XXL) $17.95

Old Turtle Audiotape $11.95

Pfeifer-Hamilton Publishers
210 West Michigan Duluth MN 55802-1908

800-247-6789